From Wages to Riches

FROM WAGES TO RICHES

For young adults who want to become financially independent

Nancy O'Hare

All rights reserved. No part of this publication may be reproduced, stored in a retrieval system or transmitted, in any form or by any means—by electronic, mechanical, photocopying, recording or otherwise—without prior written permission from the author, except by reviewers, who may quote brief passages in a review.

For permission requests, email the author at bynancyohare@gmail.com.

Published by Nancy O'Hare in 2020

Distributed by IngramSpark

ISBN: 978-1-7774017-0-2

Photography by Chad O'Hare

© 2020 by Nancy O'Hare

www.bynancyohare.com

The information in this book is true and complete to the best of the author's knowledge. All recommendations are made without guarantee on the part of the author. The author disclaims any liability in connection to the use of this information. None of the products mentioned or reviewed in this book have provided compensation to the author.

Dedication

*Dedicated to and inspired by my nieces and nephew:
Victoria, Kaela, Naomi, Liam and Geneva*

Read on to find your path to financial independence

Contents

Introduction
1

Lesson One
3

Lesson Two
4

Know This . . .
6

Lesson Three
8

Lesson Four
10

Lesson Five
12

Lesson Six
14

Lesson Seven
16

Lesson Eight
18

In Closing
19

Recommended Reading
20

About the Author
21

Introduction

In eight simple steps, learn how to best manage your money and build wealth.

Most people stumble along the way, get distracted or listen to people who would rather grow their own money than yours. This guide shows you how to avoid such pitfalls.

Personal finance is a complex topic. These lessons offer bite-sized advice to start your path towards financial prosperity. For those with enthusiasm to learn more, see the Recommended Reading section for additional resources.

By following the learnings in this book consistently, you can reach your financial goals.

Attaining financial freedom allows you to feel like the queen or king of your own castle!

Lesson One

Starting today, save at least ten percent of everything you earn

What can 10% of your wages become?

— assume a 5.5% return per year and 0.25% MER (see later lessons)

Monthly Deposit	Value in 10 Years	Value in 20 Years	Value in 30 Years
$10	$1,581	$4,250	$8,756
$100	$15,807	$42,496	$87,563
$1,000	$158,065	$424,963	$875,626

Apply this 10% rule to bonuses, extra shifts, raises, tips, another job...everything you make.
- If you earn $100, save $10.
- If you earn $1,000, save $100.
- If you earn $10,000, save $1,000.

If you can save more than 10%, *do it*!

The sooner you start saving, the sooner you can reach financial independence.

Lesson Two

Spend less than you earn

> ### Where would you spend an extra $40?
>
> *1) One extra day of budget travel in Vietnam;*
>
> *2) One dinner of pizza, cheesecake, a beverage and tip at a midrange restaurant; or,*
>
> *3) One cotton T-shirt.*
>
> *This example is meant to help you prioritize what gives you the most value. If you could only have one, which would you choose?*

Put a portion of your earnings towards expenses you need to buy. These are costs you cannot survive without: food, shelter, health care and transportation.

If not already deducted from your pay, save a portion for any taxes owed to the government. You cannot avoid taxes, so be sure to put this money in a very safe and accessible place like a high-interest savings account (HISA) with a reputable financial institution.

Spend any remaining earnings on other things you want. Remember, extra beverages, excessive clothing, fancy cars, drugs, alcohol, weekend getaways and overseas vacations are *wants*. This is all about choices. Choose what truly adds value to your life.

Patience tip: Wait for items to go on sale and get the same thing for less of your money.

Decision-making tip: It might help to ask yourself, "*what will I remember and value in one-year's time when I look back?*"

Know This...

Stock Markets are where shares of public companies are bought and sold. Most countries have a stock market for owners of businesses registered in that country who want to sell pieces of their company to other people. Pieces of the company are called stock, shares or equity.

Why do stock market movements differ from what you see happening in your local economy? Local businesses such as restaurants, gyms and trades are often not listed on the stock market. They are private businesses and their profits or losses are not picked up in public stock exchange results.

Investment-grade bonds are a type of loan thought to be fairly safe. Independent credit rating agencies rank borrowers based on their credit risk, such as AAA, AA, A or BBB. These particular ratings are all considered to be investment grade. Any lower rating is viewed to have low credit quality. *What does this mean?* A higher credit rating means the company or government borrowing money (via a bond) has a better chance of repaying you, the lender. Likewise, a low credit rating indicates the borrower is more likely to default (not repay) you, the lender.

By putting some of your money into safer *fixed income* investments, you give yourself a buffer from the ups and downs of the stock markets. Fixed income investments generally earn less money than equity, usually in the form of interest. This is your protection money.

By putting some of your money into *equities*, you give yourself the chance to grow your money and the chance to lose your money. Equity generally earns more money than fixed income over the long term, but it has more volatility (ups and downs). This is your growth money.

Exchange Traded Funds (ETFs) are collections of stocks and/or bonds that track or mimic underlying indexes or markets. *Mutual funds* are similar baskets of stocks and/or bonds that are selected by fund managers and typically have different fee structures than ETFs. For further clarification between ETFs and mutual funds, go to https://investor.vanguard.com/etf/etf-vs-mutual-fund.

Lesson Three

Decide your savings strategy

This relates to the portion of your earnings that you save from Lesson One

What are your options?

There are now options that allow you to invest in only one or two ETFs and get a completely diversified portfolio (equity and fixed income). Choose the ETFs that match your strategy (e.g., 70/30, 60/40, 50/50).

Asset allocation, asset mix, targets and strategy are terms often used interchangeably and relate to the split between equities and fixed income. It can also define where you put your money geographically.

Specific examples can be found at:

- *https://investor.vanguard.com/etf/investment-options (Americans);*
- *https://www.blackrock.com/tools/core-builder/us#/ (Americans);*
- *https://canadiancouchpotato.com/model-portfolios/ (Canadians); and,*
- *https://www.canadianportfoliomanagerblog.com/model-etf-portfolios/ (Canadians).*

Step One: Keep an emergency fund with three to six months of living expenses in a HISA.

Step Two: Choose the proportion to add to your safety net, a part you do not want to risk losing (fixed income).
- Typically 30% to 50% of your savings.
- This amount should go into investment-grade bonds, Guaranteed Investment Certificates (GICs) in Canada, Certificates of Deposit (CDs) in the United States or HISAs with reputable financial institutions.

Step Three: Choose the share to add to your riskier investments (equity).
- Typically 70% to 50% of your savings.
- This amount should go into stock markets around the world and across all industries and company sizes. For example, you may choose to put a third in your home country's stock market, a third in the United States' stock market and a third in international markets.
- The American market makes up around 44% of worldwide markets. Canada comprises less than 3%.[1]

To keep things simple, you can apply the same asset mix across all of your accounts, be it:
- RRSP, TFSA, LIRA or another account (Canadians); or,
- Roth IRA, Roth 401(k) or another account (Americans).

---

1. Based on data by the World Bank to 2018: https://data.worldbank.org/indicator/CM.MKT.LCAP.CD

Lesson Four

Buy investments that fit your strategy

Passive or Actively-Managed Fund?

For the latest results of how many actively-managed funds underperformed their benchmark (i.e., earned less than a cheaper index fund), go to Spiva S&P Indices versus Active, view 'Statistics & Reports' and then choose your country: https://us.spindices.com/spiva/#/reports.

As of June 2020, 78% of managed funds underperformed in the U.S. over the past five years (97% in Canada over the same period).

Conclusion: Evidence indicates you have a far better chance to earn more with low-cost broad-market index ETFs than in actively-managed mutual funds.

Keep costs low: They eat into your profit and amplify losses. *Management Expense Ratio* (MER)—a fund's fees—of 2% or higher is expensive, especially if there are hidden front loads, back loads (one-time fees triggered when you buy or sell) or other fees deducted from your money. Index ETFs are generally the lowest cost investments.

Be wary of complex, fancy-schmancy investments: They may be riskier, meaning you could lose much more than your cost if they do not succeed. Instead, go for straight-forward, broad-market investments that hold a mix of nearly everything in the stock market. *Broad market* means small, mid-sized and large companies across all industries.

Be wary of promises to beat the market: Investment advisors, financial planners and portfolio managers often try to sell such products that actually give them high commissions and fees out of your money. This is why they may try to talk you out of buying lower-cost funds. Research and empirical evidence show nearly no actively-managed funds do better than their comparable market index over the long term (>15 years). Seek a fee-for-service advisor who is independent and acts in your best interest.

Both ETFs and mutual funds offer *passive* and *actively-managed* alternatives. In general, passive funds charge less than actively-managed funds and ETFs typically cost less than mutual funds.

Vanguard and *iShares* offer solid fixed income and equity index ETFs. HISA, GICs in Canada and CDs in the United States are also useful fixed income options. Each have pros and cons, such as bond ETFs are more liquid (i.e., cashable) but fluctuate in value as market interest rates change.

Decision tip: Compare a bond ETF's yield to maturity (YTM) against the interest rate of a HISA, GIC or CD to see which instrument gives a better return.

Lesson Five

Avoid debt, instead save and then buy

> ### Do what *is right for YOU.*
>
> Just because other people are buying on credit does not make it smart—unless you pay off a credit card's **entire** balance every month.
>
> Interest rates might sound low, but by entering into a financing contract you lock yourself into paying for something month after month after month. Keep your freedom, save...then pay.

To save, put another 10% of your earnings into a HISA until you have saved enough to buy what you want.

Loans, credit, lines of credit, financing, payment plans, pay-later schemes, mortgages, payday loans and credit cards are all different names for the same thing: DEBT.

When you use debt, you pay more for what you want. Remember, *paying interest is not in your best interest*.

When you save and then buy, you earn interest on money while saving and then pay exactly what something is worth. Remember, *earning interest is in your best interest*.

Sometimes debt may be worth taking on. The exceptions are for a house or education. However, housing values are rising outside the affordability range in many big cities and renting may be a better option nowadays—especially if you expect to move or sell in less than 5 years. Loans for education to build your career and earn a higher paying job to repay the debt is likely worth taking on.

If you do take out debt, pay it off *as soon as possible*.

Mortgage tip: Ensure your terms allow for early payments against the principal without penalty fees.

Lesson Six

Buy low, sell high

Who can you believe?

No one can guarantee which industry, market or company will have the next big growth spurt or drop in value—no matter what someone promises. What is doing well now, may not do so in the future. What is doing poorly now, may excel in the future.

By investing in a diversified (broad-mix) portfolio, you remove the guesswork and reduce your risk. Owning a whole bunch of everything is less risky than putting your money in a select few—as the proverb says, "don't put all your eggs in one basket."

Rebalancing means selling the investment that has grown higher than its target and using that money to buy what has fallen below its target. *Or* with each pay cheque, buy the investment that is below its target percentage.
- Example: Assume your strategy was 60% equity and 40% fixed income and after a year the equity has grown to 67% while fixed income dropped to 33%. You should sell 7% of your equity and use that money to buy fixed income.

By selling when things have grown beyond their target, you *naturally sell high*. When you use those funds to buy what has fallen below its target, you are *naturally buying low*.

Pick a percentage change from your target that tells you when to rebalance your investments, like 5%. This is your trigger point. It removes the emotion and simplifies your decision.

If you only hold an all-in-one ETF, you do not have to rebalance. The ETF does it for you. The same applies when holding only one balanced mutual fund.

Do not be distracted by news of market crashes, bubbles or the latest financial market predictions.
- Money you want to use for *short-term purposes* (the next 3 to 5 years), should not be invested in the financial markets because you could lose it.
- Example: Saving for a down payment on a home or a must-have backpacking trip in Asia would be better placed in a safe liquid investment, like a HISA.
- If you are concerned about monies invested in the financial markets, *check to see if you are in balance*. If your investments are off their target by your trigger or more, then rebalance. If not, *relax*.

Lesson Seven

Take ownership of your money

What is the big deal about paying 1% more in fees?

— *assume a 6% return per year*

Monthly Deposit	Fees	Value in 10 Years[1]	Value in 20 Years[1]
$500	0.25% MER	$81,225	$225,374
$500	1.25% MER	$76,915	$200,479

[1] *If you saved $500 every month for ten years, you would **pay $3,528 more** in fees AND **earn $782 less** because the higher fees eroded your investment value. This means a total loss of **$4,310** due to a 1% increase in fees ($24,895 over 20 years). Ouch!*

Check that the financial institutions you use are protected as best they can by the government.
- Example: Many *savings* accounts, including HISAs, are protected by Federal Deposit Insurance Corporation (FDIC) in the United States or Canadian Deposit Insurance Corporation (CDIC) in Canada.
- Many *investment* accounts are similarly protected by Securities Investor Protection Corporation (SIPC) in the United States or Canadian Investor Protection Fund (CIPF) in Canada.
- These safeguards are in place to protect an individual's holdings up to a certain value in case a registered financial institution goes into liquidation or becomes insolvent (i.e., it goes bust).

Don't lose sight of your preferred retirement goals. Make sure you have a qualified financial professional build an *investment plan* (cash flow model) suited to your personal situation. It should provide a *clear roadmap* to ensure you are on track to reach your goals. Without a plan, you may need to work much longer or you may run out of money.
- A financial planner can help estimate factors like pension income, government benefits, inflation and tax impacts.
- Do this well in advance of your retirement.
- Review it once a year; you'll be surprised how motivating this knowledge can be.

Lesson Eight

Create value from whatever amount you earn

Did you know...

An average vehicle costs approximately $8,000 to $13,000 every year (portion of purchase price, maintenance, insurance and fuel). What difference would one less vehicle in your household make to your savings?

If you instead saved $8,000 annually and earned 5.75% after fees, you would have $110,209 in ten years.

Check out www.edmunds.com/tco.html (Americans) or www.car-costs.caa.ca (Canadians).

Small actions can grow to have a big impact.

Remember, you were once a tiny baby and look what you have become. Small things grow into big things.

Avoid spending what you have saved, let it keep growing.

Believe in yourself, what *you* do matters for *your* future.

In Closing

I have come to realize that many people do not know how to manage their own money. They struggle with where to start, how to sift through the volumes of information, books, journals and opinions out there.

I want to distil a path forward that everyone can follow into simple, actionable steps that you can start today.

The doorway to success may not appear quickly. However, the insights in this book give you the best chance to grow wealth through simple, actionable and proven ways that will work with dedication and time.

It is better to take your time than risk your hard-earned money on a "get-rich-quick" idea that will likely suck your money dry and force you to start over.

Stay calm during market fears and news projections about bubbles and crashes. By keeping your investments in balance with your well-diversified strategy, you are protecting your wealth and taking advantage of growth opportunities. Nothing more is needed.

I thank my husband for his attitude of continual learning, sharing knowledge and working together as a team to manage our own finances. Sure, we made mistakes along the way and those learnings are built into these lessons.

Recommended Reading

If you would like to learn more, these resources offer a comprehensive discussion about the world of personal finance. All are presented in a practical and straight-forward style.

Books

Millionaire Teacher: The Nine Rules of Wealth You Should Have Learned in School by Andrew Hallam

The Richest Man in Babylon by George S. Clason

The Wealthy Barber: The Common Sense Guide to Successful Financial Planning and *The Wealthy Barber Returns*, both by David Chilton

Online Resources

Canadian Couch Potato (blog and podcast): www.canadiancouchpotato.com

Canadian Portfolio Manager (blog and podcast): www.canadianportfoliomanagerblog.com

Vanguard Investor Tools (simulate costs, compare funds and investor questionnaire): www.vanguardcanada.ca/individual/insights/vanguard-tools.htm

About the Author

Nancy O'Hare earned an executive MBA with distinction through the Cass Business School in London, United Kingdom. She held a Chartered Professional Accountant designation for nearly twenty years before she voluntarily gave it up in good standing when she became an author. Nancy lived and worked across five continents, leading finance teams in diverse locations such as Nigeria, Oman and Switzerland. In addition to being passionate about personal finance, she is equally fascinated about travelling to remote locales and learning about disparate cultures.

Other Books by the Author

Reclaim your Financial Wits: Similar concepts for adults who want to become financially independent but have lost their way.

Searching for Unique: Kick start your travel planning with this guide / travel narrative. The author seeks to unravel our world's most unique locations, untainted by mass tourism. Explore over twenty-five amazing destinations with a focus on hiking and cultural sites.

Dust in My Pack: A travel guide and short stories in one book. Follow one traveller's journey across seven continents to reveal some of the most fascinating places to explore on our planet. Sail to Antarctica and walk among penguins or camp beneath a foraging elephant in Malawi.

www.ingramcontent.com/pod-product-compliance
Lightning Source LLC
Chambersburg PA
CBHW042236090526
44589CB00006B/79